Clubbing:

Athlete Career Killer

175 Must-know Tips for Athletes

to Avoid Violence

David L. Brown

PLAY HARD.™
DO GOOD.

CharacterAthletic.com™

ISBN-10 = 0-9826641-0-9
ISBN-13 = 978-0-9826641-0-0

First Edition – *Athlete Career Killer* ™ series of books
Published by Parkway Press, Ltd.™ Niles, Ohio
www.parkwaypress.com
Printed in the United States of America

Media Interview Contact:
David L. Brown,
Founder and President
Character Athletic, Ltd.
P.O. Box 5061
Niles, Ohio 44446-7061
United States
330-505-8113
E-mail: dlbrown88@yahoo.com

Play Hard. Do Good.™
www.CharacterAthletic.com
www.AthleteCareerKiller.com

"Excellent work! There are many lessons to be learned in your writings. The best mistakes are the ones you never make but can learn lessons from. Your look at "Clubbing and Athletes" should be used as a learner's manual for all athletes trying to find the fine line between living life and competing for a living."

Jay Crawford

Co-host - ESPN First Take

———————

"Just like any professional or college athlete would never take the field or the court without a practiced game plan, neither should they take to the social scene without proper education. Here, David has laid out the perfect game plan that all athletes need to read and embrace. Don't leave the locker-room unprepared!"

Bob Rathbun

TV voice of the NBA's Atlanta Hawks
Motivational Speaker and Author

———————

"All athletes should take note of the useful clubbing information found in this book. Athletes and the like should know the risks associated with nightlife and how their choices can affect their career and personal life forever. Taking the guidance that is in this book and working with an executive protection agency together can help protect you, your family, and your reputation from the pitfalls of a celebrity life."

Grant Linhart

President & CEO of Gideon Protective Services, Inc.
(www.executive-protection-services.net)
Current California law enforcement officer trained by retired United States Secret Service Agent Joe LaSorsa, Presidential Protection - the White House.

———————

"Where was this book before hundreds of athletes walked through a club's doors and walked out of them in trouble? This is required reading for any athlete who's a professional rookie or college freshman and a handy reference for the veteran or upperclassman who finds life's temptations tugging at him."

John Akers

Basketball Times

———————

"An absolute must read...not only for every professional athlete, but also for everyone within his or her inner circle. David has crafted a timely and invaluable handbook to help lead athletes along their best path. I look forward to sharing its lessons with all of my players."

Erica McKeon

Senior Vice President of Bruce Levy Associates International, Ltd. (BLAIL), the world's oldest agency specializing in the representation of women's pro basketball players and coaches.

———————

"David L. Brown's incisive comments concerning the lifestyle traps of clubbing and the liability issues of carrying a firearm are dead on! As a professional athlete you are one of the privileged few that made it to the show. Don't place everything you have worked so hard to obtain at risk by making poor decisions!"

Daniel W. Blake, CPO, LPI

Chief of Police (retired)
President, Aegis Security, LLC
www.aegistn.com

———————

David L. Brown

"I've spent the last 30 years educating people to become better athletes through mental preparation and understanding the psychological aspects of competition. David L. Brown provides necessary preparation skills to keep athletes from making devastating mistakes off the playing fields and courts. I highly recommend his books as guidance for all athletes' emotional and physical well-being. The POPs system empowers the athlete to take control of their life away from competition and keep them out of harm's way."

Mike Margolies

Sports Psychology Consultants

TheMental-Game.com

"With clarity, logic and great insight, David L. Brown has produced a highly credible roadmap to assist today's modern professional and college athletes by shedding light on a wide array of off the field and court challenges, disasters and mishaps. This book is long overdue and is a must-read."

Forrest Dorsett

Founder & Principal Dorsett Sports Marketing

www.dorsettsportsmarketing.com

Clubbing: Athlete Career Killer

"Clubbing: Athlete Career Killer, addresses many of the dangers college and professional athletes encounter when they indulge in city nightlife. This book is a must read for all athletes due to the serious and sometimes deadly consequences that can result from a night out on the town."

Shaun Tyrance

Sport Psychology Consultant

University of North Carolina at Charlotte

---

*"David L. Brown's Clubbing: Athlete Career Killer is on a level that ANY athlete should read. As an athlete takes that NEXT step into their future, they should keep in mind, *ALL* organizations have people watching you 24/7. If you learn ANYTHING from reading this book know this : **Think BIG so you can become BIGGER.**"*

James Heintz

Director of Football Operations

Elite Sports Agency

www.theelitesportsagency.com

David L. Brown

"David Brown's "Clubbing: Athlete's Career Killer" is definitely a book athletes who want to "WIN" in the sport of life should read! For the past 25 years, I have had the pleasure of spanning the globe coaching, consulting and helping amazing athletes (amateur/college/pro/superstars), teams, clubs and companies achieve their highest and best levels of SUCCESS in all walks of Life (sports, fitness, business & life). Congratulations, David, these valuable life lessons and athlete blueprints for success can and will help them ignite their champion within and live their legacy."

Joy Macci, PhD

CEO/International Tennis Specialist
Author/Speaker/Superstar Success Coach
www.JoyofSport.com

"'Clubbing: Athlete Career Killer' is a great read and playbook full of tips for athletes to either avoid or (if necessary) deal with public situations where people wish to antagonize them, or worse. The examples David Brown gives

are great depictions of real life circumstances that athletes find themselves in. David doesn't want guys to live as shut-ins, but simply to have a plan and realize the importance of practicing that plan just as they would practice during their playing careers. It's a great resource for both college and professional athletes."

Anthony Herron

Former professional football player and championship winning coach. Current television analyst for both the NFL Network and Big Ten Network. President and Co-Founder of Life Success for Athletes, a company geared toward helping athletes avoid off field hurdles and pitfalls that await them upon leaving college.

Athletes will enjoy reading, and benefit from the valuable information in the author's *Athlete Career Killer*™ series:

Clubbing: Athlete Career Killer™

Drunk Driving: Athlete Career Killer™

Guns: Athlete Career Killer™

Drugs: Athlete Career Killer™

Domestic Violence: Athlete Career Killer™

Infidelity: Athlete Career Killer™

Home Invasion: Athlete Career Killer™

Gambling: Athlete Career Killer™

Money: Athlete Career Killer ™

College Academics: Athlete Career Killer™

POPS™: Athlete Career Savior™

3RD Down and God: #1 Spiritual Guide for Athletes™

The author believes that in addition to this book series being placed in the hands of all professional athletes, each and every freshman student athlete, in every recruiting class, who commits to continue his athletic and academic career at a college or university program, should also be handed the Athlete Career Killer™ book series upon signing. The same with every draft class in the NFL, NBA, NHL, and Major League Baseball. "Welcome — here's our gift to you."

Dedicated to my wonderful children,

Alýssa and Brandon.

"Thank you for inspiring me and keeping me young at heart. You are the future leaders of our country. I am so proud of you. I love you very much."

Dad!

To all athletes…

"The economy is in a recession. Your character shouldn't be."

David L. Brown

Acknowledgments

I give honor and praise to God. Without Him, nothing would be possible.

To my late father, Jimmy Brown. You taught me how to be a man. You taught me character and integrity, even when the world was chipping at my heels. You are gone, but forever remain in my heart.

To my late sister Buena; your giving heart and spirituality live with me each day and resonates true because of you.

To my mother Doris; thank you for always telling me I could do anything I put my mind to, no matter what.

To my sister Sharon; thank you for always believing in me.

To my brother Jim; thank you for all your support and encouragement.

To my niece Danae; your laughter and easy smile make for brighter days.

To friends, family, and colleagues; thank you for your encouragement, motivation, patience, and insights.

To all athletes who conduct themselves in a professional manner and who do the right things by making good choices in your lives and athletic careers. You have my utmost respect and admiration.

Many thanks to editors Jim and Sue Long for your excellent work and professionalism. It was a pleasure working with you. For more information about their editing prowess, go to www.agoodedit.com

Contents

Introduction

Athlete Disaster Formula

Welcome to the most volatile formula in sports.
College or pro athlete + nightclub + alcohol + 2:00 - 3:00
a.m. + guns + drinking and driving = Big trouble!

I wrote this book specifically to help with the safety
and education of all athletes who participate in nightlife.
Note that when I refer to the term "clubbing," it is meant
to include ALL venues of nightlife; nightclubs, bars, strip
clubs, other gentleman's clubs, and parties.

It is imperative that I begin by telling you that about
98% of college and professional athletes combined are
upstanding citizens of good character, and DO NOT
cause legal, or other problems!

Unfortunately, I GUARANTEE THIS…

As I write this, Saturday, June 20, 2009, an athlete somewhere is making a poor decision, knowingly or not, that will be heard and read about on the web and on your favorite sports network within the next 48 hours (if not sooner)…I GUARANTEE IT!

Since you are holding this book in your hands right now, you, no doubt, have an interest in reclaiming your sanity, peace of mind, and confidence when venturing out into nightlife. And, I'd like to help. As an athlete, you've heard about the sad stories, and have seen the unfortunate headlines regarding your peers. You probably know a teammate right now who's made some poor choices and suffered the consequences. Maybe your team or the league brought someone in to talk to you about the dangers lurking in the night, but it only covered generalities, and you find yourself still looking over your shoulder in fear of the unknown. Basically, anywhere you go where alcohol is being served — this book is for you.

You have good reason to be fearful. Clubbing can be scary and violent — unless you have the right tools and techniques. You don't have to feel like there's a "bullseye" on your back 24-7. It's a problem desperately searching for the right solution. This book provides athletes a fresh, comprehensive solution for what you think you know, and what you've already been told. It's an innovative and specialized way to approach the potential life-threatening nightlife problems you face in today's society.

My job is to help you, as an athlete, stay safe, and allow you to keep playing the game you love. You can't help your team win if you make bad decisions when clubbing or otherwise, and later find yourself dealing with police, defense attorneys, courts, judges, prosecutors, and potential team and league suspensions. Getting into trouble can happen in an instant — but the legal process can take much longer.

Because of this, athletes who attend clubs MUST have an effective security plan in place BEFORE, DURING, and AFTER you go clubbing, and potentially encounter obnoxious or intoxicated patrons who want to cause trouble. Much is written in the media about athletes making poor decisions, but there are few solutions that offer the total package to help them stay safe when clubbing... until now. I don't just want to talk about your safety — I want to *show* you how to stay safe... step by step.

Later, I reveal my techniques and tips called POPS™, that will allow you to increase your awareness and confidence RIGHT NOW! You can't take for granted any longer that you'll know what to do or how to react during a potentially violent situation. I guarantee my tips and techniques will serve as extremely valuable tools for all athletes throughout your career and post-career. Your chances of success in using this book are greater when you exhibit an open mind and a willingness to learn.

Part One

Part One

Chapter 1

Clubbing™ Can Kill

Many of the POPS tips and techniques I created for this book I tested myself — and they work. They'll work for you too — if used properly and consistently. Just like a rookie NFL athlete doesn't completely know the offense or defense during his first mini-camp and OTAs (organized team activities), the more repetitions he gets, the more he'll learn. The more he learns, the better he'll become. The more confident he gets, the faster he'll play, and the more productive he'll be on the field.

The reason I began to do research for this book started with a sad story I saw on ESPN in mid-December, 2006, involving a former high profile Chicago Bears defensive tackle. Later, the news of athletes, nightclubs, guns, violence, and drinking and driving kept coming and coming, to the point I realized I needed to write this book.

It was reported that Chicago police searched for a man who allegedly harassed the Bear's athlete on a nightclub dance floor, on an early Saturday morning, sparking a fight that resulted in the shooting death of his boyhood friend and bodyguard. His friend died after the fight inside a popular club in the trendy River North neighborhood, police said.

Witnesses told police that another man repeatedly bumped into the athlete on the dance floor, a source familiar with the investigation told the *Chicago Tribune*. The athlete's friend and bodyguard intervened, the newspaper reported, struck the man, and both fell to the floor. When club security pulled them apart, the other man pulled out a gun and shot and killed the athlete's friend, witnesses said.

* * *

To prepare for this book, I went clubbing in Cleveland and Pittsburgh every other weekend for three months. I saw drunks, druggies, women with agendas, men with agendas, the "hustle" of men trying to hook up with women and vice-versa. I saw the liars, the dealers, the phonies, the pretenders, the con-men and women, and the game players — all a part of the dynamic nocturnal playground known as urban nightlife. Many of the clubs I attended were in nice neighborhoods and considered upper-middle class to upscale.

The clubbing vibe I experienced during my research was exhilarating, yet scary...sexy...yet shallow. It provided a two-to-three hour short-term "escape" from the everyday hum drum. The pressure on males in clubs, bars, and parties is enormous, depending on your motives. The direct competition for women is silently fierce, yet forcefully felt. In one example, a woman approached me at the club. I said goodbye at hello™. I sensed she was high on something.

Most of the experiences left me feeling fortunate to leave safe and sound and without incident. Some other club customers weren't so lucky. I witnessed several fights in parking lots after the clubs closed, a fight or two inside the club between guys, and women fist-fighting other women outside. I heard the echo of shots being fired outside the clubs and that eerie sound of police and ambulance sirens raging against the early morning air. Incidents like these didn't occur every time I went clubbing, but each time I could sense emotions could potentially erupt at any time, anywhere, over the slightest thing.

We all like to party sometimes. When you're an athlete, it's an understandable major rush for you. You're in great shape. You look good, and so, of course, the ladies are going to dig you. You're also a star on the field or on the court, and people gravitate toward that. They want to feel like they're a part of it, and so you may get a huge rush from that experience. Athletes want to be loved, accepted, appreciated, understood, and acknowledged. It's okay — it's part of simple human nature.

There are a ton of reasons why you want to go clubbing — some you might not even be aware of. I'm going to dive into those reasons shortly. For now, I just want you to start becoming aware that you have to make good choices when you decide to go out for a night.

Take, for example, the tendency of some professional athletes to carry a gun. They do so, they say, for protection. And, granted, they have a point. No one wants to be a target, and many athletes are. There are too many examples of athletes going to jail because they used their gun, or someone used a gun on them.

Athletes must always consider this when entering a nightclub, strip club, bar, or late night party: If you believe you have legitimate reasons to carry a gun into any of the above-mentioned places...the other guy does too! You're probably not the only one packin' for protection. Multiply one person by maybe ten to fifteen in a club and you can see how there may be a potential problem if things get out of hand, especially when alcohol is involved.

33

The sad fact is, if you make a poor decision, the world will know. I've done a study on it. Nightclubs and bars can be exciting and fun for athletes to attend, but with that comes special problems. As you can imagine, an urban club or bar that markets itself to young adults in an attempt to become the next "hot" place to be is bound to have a few conduct problems. Before you take one step inside a nightclub, bar, strip club, or late night party, reflect on the potential dangers and consequences and ask yourself...is it really worth it?

Sometimes people bring outside conflicts and jealousies into a club that can erupt into violence. Athletes need to know how to handle themselves if they get angry, or if they encounter obnoxious or intoxicated people who want to cause trouble. And that's what this book is all about. I respect you as an athlete. I'm a former blue chip athlete and college football player, and I know the kind of dedication and commitment it takes to be on a team. I want to help you keep your career intact and not be potentially ruined or tarnished because you didn't have the right tools to take with you to a club to prevent possible disaster from happening.

I designed a simple to follow, but very effective program called POPS™. POPS stands for PO'd Points.™ (also Pissed Off Points™). Until now, you've been told to be responsible, to make sure that target on your back isn't too big and bold, but you haven't had a plan. POPS gives you a clubbing game plan. It's one that could save your life — literally.

As an athlete, you have a C.H.O.I.C.E™, and it's based on...

C.ourage

H.onesty

O.pportunity

I.ntegrity

C.ommitment

E.xcellence

You will learn in this book how to recognize potential dangers while clubbing, and the "career killers" they can be. POPS will also give you a stronger voice to speak out when you see a teammate about to make a bad decision — like drinking and driving, and other potentially dangerous choices.

Chapter 2

Ugly Headline

Turn your wounds into wisdom.

Oprah Winfrey

Pop! Pop! Pop!

You're all familiar with the sound of a gun fired — and the headlines that follow. Top athlete goes out and gets drunk, or high, gets in his car and something awful happens. He's shot. He gets into a fight. He is faced with potentially losing his career.

Take the story of a Louisville wide receiver. It was late at night on a fourth of July weekend in 2008. He's out with his fiancé. They just had a fun night of clubbing, and they're walking to their car. The next thing he knows he's being shot at. Nineteen times. It happens in a parking garage, so there's nowhere to hide.

By the grace of God, only one of those nineteen bullets hits him. But it's in the back, and his playing days may be over. The athlete told a reporter he wasn't sure why it happened or how it happened, but he is thankful he survived. He said he was at the club when someone inappropriately touched his fiancé. Words were exchanged. When he left the club, he was followed and later attacked outside a parking garage.

He later said to a reporter, "The doctors said an inch to the right it would have hit my spine, an inch to the left it would have hit a vital organ." Fortunately, doctors were able to remove the bullet shortly after the attack. He's one of the lucky ones. He's going to be able to return to the game. He gets to play again, but he also gets to live the rest of his life with that awful memory. The athlete said he's more cognizant that when he, friends and teammates go out, people know them and things like shootings shouldn't happen, but sometimes they do.

"We just have to watch what we do," he said.

He will always carry the scar in the middle of his back as a painful reminder of how quickly things can change. How many athletes can you name who have been injured or killed after a night of clubbing? How many athletes can you name who have gotten arrested? How many can you name who got into a fight, hurt someone, got suspended, or lost their career because of it? One is too many. It's the risk you take when you decide to go out for a night of clubbing.

You, as an athlete and human being, and those who are with you at the time, CAN, unknowingly or not, greatly contribute to an escalated and potentially violent situation while clubbing! My POPS tips and techniques will help you avoid possible escalated problems, and I'll tell you how saying just two simple words repeatedly could possibly save your life.

Chapter 3

Shots Fired

During the early morning hours on January 19, 2009, in Midland, Texas, a Sul Ross State running back was shot and killed at a nightclub.

According to public police reports, the athlete died "…after he was shot multiple times in the body and the legs," just before 4:00 a.m. at the Pleasures Club, said Sgt. Lupe Bretado of the Midland Police Department. He was 23, and died at Midland Memorial Hospital.

Three people were later charged, each with one count of murder. The athlete was a star running back at Permian High School before going to Sul Ross, the *Odessa American* reported Monday in its online edition. He rushed for 909 yards on 152 carries and scored 10 touchdowns in his first season with the Lobos, making the American Southwest All-Conference team.

* * *

Athletes at all levels — high school, college and the professional ranks — are perpetuating or finding themselves victims of violence at an increasingly alarming rate. What makes this even more upsetting is that when most people hear that an athlete was shot in the wee hours after a party, they don't wonder about his race. Most don't want to admit that, for the most part, we are talking about African American athletes.

The logical question is why this continues at such a startling rate — and what can be done to curtail it. The next question is why African-American athletes find themselves disproportionately involved in violence. I'm not looking to blame the victim, I just think that this issue needs to be explored, discussed and addressed head-on. Athletes of all races at some point in their careers go out and have a good time. On the face of things, there's nothing wrong with this. Should it be that different from a factory worker wanting to blow off some steam on a Friday night?

Unfortunately, under the surface, there exists a culture that glorifies violence and danger in many of the venues that these athletes choose. "Kickin it" with homies from the block that might have ties to the street game is alluring and dangerous — and may seem to help these athletes maintain their "street credibility" off the field.

Athletes often quickly find themselves in a tense environment — competing for women and becoming a potential target for others trying to prove something. After a few drinks, tempers may flare, punches get thrown and weapons are brought into the mix.

Adding to the situation is that African Americans typically socialize in environments that blur economic or class lines. A number of African-Americas are the first members of their families to graduate from college or land an attractive career. By leaving the neighborhood, they may return to face a certain stigma, or feel the need to overcompensate to "fit in" with their old friends.

What are the choices? To run the risk of having their ethnicity challenged because they went off to school? This accomplishment may cause them perceived as being "too good" to hang out with the very people they grew up with — some of whom have taken markedly different directions with their lives.

Unfortunately, the athletes and scholars that we send off to school often find themselves without a support system when they return home. This is one of the first places that we, as a society, fall down. Millions of words have been written about the challenges African-Americans face when they excel at something, but it's time to do more than write about it. When we don't support them, an atmosphere ripe for violence grows. Athletes bear the brunt of this because they are more exposed, more celebrated and often targeted.

While the questions around why this violence continues are simple, the answers are not. It's a complex issue that will not go away without some serious dialogue. I don't have all the answers, but it's time to start asking the questions more loudly, forcing our communities to ensure that more African-American athletes are given room to succeed without the threat of violence, murder and destruction.

Chapter 4

Responsibility

"You can avoid your responsibilities, but you can't avoid the consequences of avoiding your responsibilities."

Famous moral axiom

If someone has been drinking at a club, bar, or party, DO NOT look at them funny, DO NOT stare them down, DO NOT talk to their girl or look her up and down, DO NOT contribute in any way, shape, or form, to a situation which might cause a dude to act a fool toward you...or you toward him, the police or others. I'll show you later how POPS can help you keep your emotions in check.

From the NFL

Tragic Circumstance

A Jacksonville Jaguars offensive tackle was shot and critically wounded outside an apartment building in September 2008, as he and a former teammate waited for two women they had met earlier at a nightclub, police said.

The athlete, then 26, and another athlete were waiting in a Cadillac Escalade when a gunman fired into the vehicle, said Jacksonville Sheriff's Office spokesman Ken Jefferson. The athlete was shot several times, but it wasn't clear where he was hit. The shooting happened around 2:45 a.m. in a middle to upper middle-class neighborhood just west of downtown Jacksonville. The players had gone to the apartment complex so the women could drop off their car, authorities said. The women, who appeared to be in their twenties, declined comment when they were escorted by police back to the complex.

A 6'-7", 345-pound linemen, the athlete was the third NFL player to be shot in the past 18 months. A Washington Redskins star safety was fatally shot during what police said was a botched burglary attempt at his Miami-area home in November. A Denver Broncos cornerback was killed when his rented limousine was sprayed with bullets minutes after leaving a New Year's party at a club in 2007.

The Jacksonville Jaguar athlete is now paralyzed below the waist, and one leg had to be amputated. Doctors said he suffered fourteen bullet wounds to the back, left groin, left leg, and right buttock. In addition, a bullet severed his spinal cord, causing the paralysis. The amputation was the result of damage to his left leg and groin, where blood clots formed. Five bullets alone were removed from his urinary bladder and the twenty-six-year-old athlete also had bouts of pneumonia, infections and renal failure. He has undergone physical therapy to learn how to move from his bed to a wheelchair. He will never walk again, a doctor said. "He has extreme grief for a lifetime of dreams he won't be able to fulfill," his agent told reporters.

* * *

Professional and college athletes being victimized by violent crime — or perpetrating it — is becoming a major social issue. In many ways, this has become a lifestyle issue. The lines are no longer clear — the above-mentioned Jaguar athlete was shot in a nice neighborhood. He and a former teammate had been at a club (presumably a nice one) and were returning to the home of two women they met while they were out. It's a delicate issue. Obviously, the person or people who pulled the trigger are the criminals here, and the Jaguar athlete is the victim. But athletes are finding there's a pattern to a lot of the trouble.

These athletes are seemingly being targeted at nightclubs. Is the atmosphere at clubs, bars and parties so charged that any small slight, any suggestive look can result in murder? I say yes. There doesn't always have to be a reason, and the problem isn't limited to high-profile athletes. Does this have the potential to turn pro athletes into hermits? Will it ramp up the idea that every athlete needs a posse, and those posses need to be armed at least as well as the bad guys doing the targeting?

48

Every sports league runs rookie seminars that go over possible scenarios. Clearly, young professional athletes should be able to go out for dinner and a few drinks wherever they want. But it's just as clear that alcohol, egos, women, and late nights/early mornings fuse to create a highly combustible compound.

One thing, and maybe only one, is for sure: this is no longer just an image problem for a team or a league. This is a problem that is drifting perilously close to becoming a crisis, if it hasn't already reached that point. And, it's time to focus on how it affects the young men involved, and give them the opportunity of a plan, before, during, and after clubbing.

I hope young athletes are reading this and thinking, *You know, maybe I shouldn't go out to the clubs.* There's always going to be someone who is jealous, crazy or off-balance mentally, and if you get into altercations, anything can and will happen. But if clubbing you must — club responsibly, and take POPS with you. If you're making hundreds of thousands of dollars with your body, you better take care of it and do your best not to put it in harm's way. You can still have fun — just don't go places where you know inebriated, rowdy people will be around competing for women and attention.

If an athlete is truly concerned about being a target, as well they should, what with being public figures and celebrities, I'm all for you becoming aware of that potential threat. But, if you think you're a target, and you're trying to avoid being a target, then please don't go to a place where you might become target practice. Let's be honest, a nightclub, for example, is the last place an athlete should go to A-V-O-I-D being a target.

More from the NFL

"Character is made by many acts; it may be lost by a single one."
Unknown

A Cleveland Browns wide receiver was charged with killing a pedestrian last month while driving drunk after a night out at a swank South Beach nightclub on April 1, 2009, in Miami. An arrest warrant charging him, age twenty-eight, with DUI manslaughter was filed in the March 14, 2009 accident that killed a fifty-nine-year-old man. The athlete's blood-alcohol level after the crash was .126, well above Florida's legal limit of .08, according to results of a blood test. It was later determined he also had marijuana in his system at the time of the accident. He was also charged with DUI, which carries a possible six-month sentence, plus fines and community service for first offenders.

"Whenever a deadly accident occurs and a driver is impaired, families suffer," Miami-Dade States Attorney Katherine Fernandez Rundle said in a statement. "I can only repeat this message over and over: if you are going to drink, don't drive."

An additional police affidavit filed Wednesday said that on the morning of the crash, the athlete was drinking at a nightclub in a posh hotel on South Beach. He left to go to a nearby home. The athlete later agreed to plead guilty to a DUI manslaughter charge, and also reached a financial settlement with the deceased man's family to avoid a potential lawsuit.

The athlete served twenty-four days of a thirty-day jail sentence. Shortly after his guilty plea, he was suspended indefinitely, without pay, by NFL commissioner, Roger Goodell.

Through excerpts of a letter released by the NFL, Goodell wrote: "The conduct reflected in your guilty plea resulted in the tragic loss of life and was inexcusable. While the criminal justice system has determined the legal consequences of this incident, it is my responsibility as NFL commissioner to determine appropriate league discipline for your actions, which have caused irreparable harm to the victim and his family, your club, your fellow players and the NFL."

Chapter 5

A Big Gun Story You Probably Heard About

Guns are NOT your Friend

A Miami Dolphins linebacker defends athletes' need for guns...

In an interview that was aired on "ESPN First Take" in 2008, the Dolphins linebacker said some NFL players feel the need to have a firearm to defend themselves and their families. "Everybody has their mistakes, but that's exactly what they are.... Until you've been in that situation, when you've been robbed at gunpoint, or you've had a gun waved in your face, or had your house broken into before, or been carjacked, you really don't know what it's like," he told a reporter.

A well known former New York Giant wide receiver was injured in the early morning hours of November 29, 2008, in a nightclub in Manhattan, when a .40-caliber Glock he was carrying in his waistband slipped down his leg and, as he grabbed at it, he accidentally pulled the trigger and shot himself in the thigh. The Giants suspended the athlete for the final four games of the regular season and placed him on the non-football injury list. He was released by the team in April 2009. As of this writing, he has not yet been disciplined by the NFL, and his charge of criminal possession of a weapon has been postponed until September 2009.

The Dolphin linebacker had his own scare on Aug. 30, 2003, when he was with the Pittsburgh Steelers. He decided to fly out to see Colorado State, his alma mater, face Colorado. Afterward, he went to a Denver bar with some friends and, while standing in a parking lot with about 150 other people, got caught in the middle of a shooting.

Denver police said the athlete was an innocent bystander, and that the shooting, which left one dead and five others wounded, was possibly gang related. The athlete was struck in the buttocks by a .9 mm bullet, which lodged in his right thigh.

"When you get out of a situation like that, and you've been in harm's way, the first thing that goes through your mind is, I'd rather get caught and take the little penalty from the media, whatever the situation may be, than not have a chance to save my life," he later told a reporter. "It's tough out there, so I'm not gonna say I condone what happened. It was a mistake being there."

The Dolphin linebacker said he does not have a bodyguard, but acknowledged that he owns a firearm, and has a permit to carry a concealed weapon in California, but not in Florida. "I'm not saying I'm walking down the street with a handgun on my hip," he said. "I'm not doing it for show. It's not fun. Hopefully, in my lifetime, I never have to use it."

NFL commissioner Roger Goodell, who discussed the situation, said the NFL has a strict gun policy but also must manage it against the constitutional right to bear arms.

"The real issue to me, is when the players feel they're unsafe, they shouldn't be there," Goodell told reporters.

"So get out, don't be there. If you feel the need to have a firearm to be some place, you're in the wrong place."

* * *

No one is suggesting that players become prisoners in their homes and avoid the public. Young men like to go to clubs to relax, but they have to be smart about it. A loaded gun in a public place is never the answer.

As a world-renowned scholar and purveyor of human behavior, USC sociology professor Todd Boyd has clearly come to recognize all distinctions.

"For me, part of this controversy lies in the ignored reality that there lies a twisted push for gun rights all across this country," Boyd told a reporter. "Right after the Obama election, all you heard about were all the people who were going out buying weapons in anticipation of amended gun laws. I'm not defending athletes, but people still want to signal out and separate athletes — particularly black athletes — when they're involved in these kinds of incidents when the reality is there's a huge gun culture that exists within our entire population."

NFL Players Share Thoughts on Guns
2008

"We're not like Joe or Sally. We definitely have a big red target on our backs. They know our salaries. You can go on web sites and find our salaries. I just never go anywhere alone. I just try to be with people who I know are thinking security first."

* * *

"My message is… 'If you have to go somewhere where you feel you've got to carry a handgun, you don't need to be going to that spot. Let us help you go somewhere else.' … We had a little, let me say, dip in the thing or a blip on the radar there for a bit, but I just wanted to remind the guys to keep doing things as pros and be smart, and understand, don't take your life, your career and other things at risk."

* * *

"It's real. People are allowed to carry guns, it's in the Constitution. So people want to protect themselves. But you've got to do it legally."

* * *

"The whole country has a problem. No education on them, and people can buy them anywhere now, off the street, and don't have to have a license or anything. I think when it's done the right way, and you know about it, and you register it, then it's okay. But you get guns in the wrong people's hands, it's a problem."

* * *

A Houston Texans director of security said, "We discourage guys from having guns, but if they choose to own guns, handguns, we just make sure they get the proper training, that they're licensed so they're carrying it legally. We also have (Houston police) officers come in and talk to the guys about gun safety, and just gun awareness. Make sure that they know that most of the time, having a gun in a situation just escalates the situation, where not having a gun might not lead to a drastic outcome."

* * *

"I've just never been in a circumstance where I've felt that (lack of security). It's never happened to me or my family. But you know people know where you live or where you're gonna be. If someone wants to get to you, they can. That's when you start feeling a little scared."

* * *

One player commented on why NFL players carry guns, "Why not? Everybody else is. It's all right to have possession to protect ourselves. We're a high target. We have plenty of people who point us out. They know where we live. They

59

know exactly when we're gone. They know exactly what our schedule is. They know exactly what we make because it's printed out every year. We are a target. Our whole business, our personal life and professional life, is always out there in the media. So why not?"

* * *

"Unfortunately, the NFL is a microcosm of society, so, of course, there are going to be some guys out there who are into guns and into the extremes just because it is maybe looked at as being cool. That's the unfortunate part of it. With maturity that changes, but you're talking about twenty to twenty-one-year-old guys who come into this league."

* * *

A wide receiver told the story that when he was nine years old, his older brother was shot and ended up a paraplegic. He stated, "It's heavy on my heart that an athlete has to feel that uncomfortable to carry a weapon with him. You hate to see guys in such a silly situation."

* * *

"As an athlete, you always have extra scrutiny to whom much is given, much is expected, so you have to understand the position you're in and carry yourself accordingly."

* * *

"If I'm going somewhere by myself, if I'm going out or something, I'm going to have security and have somebody with me. I'm not going to do it myself, but to each his own."

* * *

"You can't bring a knife to a gunfight, so sometimes you think you have to protect yourself with a gun. Me, personally, that's not something I want to do, but some guys feel that way, and not that it's right or wrong, but you've got to protect yourself. You should be able to go out and have a good time as well."

* * *

"Personally if I've got to carry a gun, I don't need to go out to public. It's probably a place I shouldn't be at. Playing in Pittsburgh, the way the city and fans are one, I don't think we have a need for that. Always when you go out, you need to be aware of your surroundings and what not."

* * *

"We've got to continue to educate ourselves. We can't get bored, saying 'That's the same old message.' Sometimes it may take two or three times for the message to register. That's just life. We've got to keep reinforcing player safety. Choosing the right place to be, the right time of night, etc. We've got to realize we are part of society's rules on top of the NFL's. That keeps us in the same fish bowl."

* * *

"That's the no-win situation when we get attacked by someone in a club. Do we fight back, standing a chance of getting sued? Do you fight back and stand a chance of somebody looking for you after the club or the next few weeks looking for you? Or do you just take it?"

* * *

"Any time that you introduce a gun into any situation, that's a scary situation, no matter what it is. The scary thing is, that a lot of these guys don't understand or don't know how to use a gun. It's new to them. They think, 'Shoot first, ask questions later.'"

* * *

"If you're an NFL player and you go out in public or you go out on the town, you're a target. Women come up to you. Guys want to challenge you to show how tough they are. If you're going to be out there, you have to learn how to walk away from situations. Too many young players haven't learned how to do that."

Chapter 6

Headlines Athletes Don't Want

"Avoiding a fight is a mark of honor; only fools insist on quarreling."

Proverbs 20:3, NLT

A New Orleans Saints defensive end posted $10,000 bond on May 22, 2008 in Blakely, Georgia, after his indictment on an involuntary manslaughter charge stemming from a February nightclub fight in which a woman died.

The athlete himself was stabbed in the neck during the February 3 fight. He was charged by a Grand Jury that also charged another person with felony murder and killing a fetus in the shooting death of another woman at the club, who was pregnant. She died after being taken to the Southeast

Alabama Medical Center in Dothan. The athlete and another person had allegedly gone to a club in Blakely, not far from the player's hometown of Colquitt, and somehow got entangled in the fight.

* * *

On June 18, 2008, an Arizona Cardinals running back was among five people arrested after a fight at a nightclub in Rocky Mount, North Carolina. Police said an off-duty officer called for assistance around 1:30 a.m. Wednesday after the fight broke out at the nightclub. The then twenty-five-year-old athlete was charged with disorderly conduct.

* * *

It was determined on June 26, 2008, that a Detroit Lions' top draft pick would serve one year of probation and pay $52,000 in medical expenses after settling an assault charge stemming from a 2007 bar brawl that resulted in a patron being seriously injured, according to *The Boston Globe*.

The 6'-7" athlete and a former college teammate, were both charged with assault and battery with a dangerous weapon for their roles in the brawl. The charges against them would be dismissed if they completed the terms of their probation and stayed out of trouble as part of the settlement they reached with an injured patron.

It was alleged that the athlete and his former teammate intervened in a dispute between the bar's co-owner and a patron. The co-owner, a Massachusetts State Police Sergeant, wanted the patron and his friends to move so the athlete and a group of his teammates could sit down, *The Globe* reported.

According to *The Globe* report, the patron, a software engineer, testified during a preliminary hearing that the athlete grabbed him in a two-arm choke hold and dragged him across the bar's dance floor while two other athletes repeatedly punched him. The patron also testified that he and the athlete crashed into a table and that he lapsed in and out of consciousness while the athlete and another person kicked him. The patron suffered a broken neck and other injuries, according to the report.

Chapter 7

The NFL Commissioner Speaks

June 25, 2007

PALM BEACH GARDENS, Fla.

After commissioner Roger Goodell spoke to rookies for about ten minutes about making good decisions, a Washington Redskins rookie quarterback asked an innocent yet telling question: "What exactly can we do?"

The simple answer: Think. But in the complex world of the NFL, where instant money meets youth in an environment that mixes sports and corporate life, asking people to think isn't always easy.

"This is about the decisions they are going to have to make, and this is a big transition from college," Goodell told a reporter. "I think we're providing some tools for them, but the big focus for us is how do we expand this? How do we make it better? We want to continually promote these messages and help the players make good choices.

"I'd be naïve to think that everyone is going to understand this and that we're not going to have any discipline matters going forward. But again, I think we are making the players more aware of the standards of behavior and, secondly, we're giving them more tools and resources to make better decisions. Hopefully, that's going to have a great impact."

"The man means business," said a New England Patriots safety and former University of Miami standout, who was involved in a shooting before his final season, and involved in a brawl during that campaign to a reporter. "If you get in trouble now, it's because you don't care."

Goodell told reporters that players becoming targets was "a big issue." "We have to do everything we can to educate our players of the simple things they can do to protect themselves."

A former Cleveland Browns head coach, also speaking at the event, provided his perspective to athletes, touching on numerous issues, from dealing with fans, to the media, to family, to women. "If you have a wife, you don't need a girlfriend," he told the athletes. "If you have a girlfriend, one is enough."

Chapter 8

Anywhere, Anytime

No matter where professional athletes are — at home, out with friends, in their cars, in a limo — they know they could be targets. They, perhaps, have never been more uneasy about their personal safety than they are right now.

"There's no question we're targets," said a Chicago Bears tight end to a reporter. "We're high-profile people. They want what you have, and they're willing to do whatever they have to do to get it."

One NBA forward told a reporter, "You always want to feel like you're safe, but that doesn't seem to be the case anymore. If these things keep happening like they're happening, you'd be a fool not to take necessary measures to protect yourself and your family."

That's a point each professional sports league has been making for years, be it at annual rookie symposiums or in constant updates from league and team security personnel throughout the season.

Robert Gadson, head of security for the NBA Player's Association, sent a memo to all NBA players, urging them to review their security procedures and scrutinize everything from the height of the bushes in front of their homes to the people with whom they surround themselves to the type of home security system they have.

"Our players, their work schedule is public knowledge, the amount of money they make is public knowledge, they're easily recognizable and they're rich," said Gadson, who spent 23 years as a New York police detective.

Even if athletes aren't targeted more often than the average man on the street, extra security might provide a sense of calm for college and professional athletes. After all, we live in an internet driven society. All sorts of personal information — someone's phone number, address, or even a satellite image of an athlete's house — can be found on the Web. And once your salary increases, so does the anxiety.

A two-time Super Bowl quarterback's public persona isn't limited to game days. Does his being a high- profile athlete give fans an invitation into his life? If there's a line that shouldn't be crossed, where is it? With no easy answers, this high profile QB is one of a growing number of athletes who uses bodyguards when going out. He told a reporter that, much like in a collapsing pocket, you sometimes can't tell what's coming until it's too late. He spoke about the time he found himself alone, and it was scary. He said he didn't have anybody with him, when suddenly a guy brandished a weapon in his face. The QB said he tried to keep his cool and talked his way out of it. People later showed up and helped him get rid of the guy. That's when he said he decided to have someone with him all the time.

73

Having a bodyguard doesn't make you weak. I'm sure 99% of the guys in the NFL could take care of themselves in a fight. The issue is protecting yourself and what you have — your name, health, family, money. An athlete might go a whole lifetime and not encounter one thing. Or you may encounter ten things in one weekend. You never know.

Security doesn't mean a guy holding your hand as you're walking through a crowd. They're just there to keep an eye out. You have to interact with people. You have to shake hands, say hello, take pictures, give autographs. You can't always be watching what people are doing behind you, and there's been more than one occasion when an athlete was grateful to have a security guy — or two, with him.

Chapter 9

Choices

"The only difference between where you are right now and where you'll be next year, at this same time, are the choices you make."

David L. Brown

Will you take the knowledge this book offers and apply it — right now? Or will you just blow it off? Make the right C.H.O.I.C.E. and stay safe. Know that precaution guarantees nothing.

A late Denver Bronco cornerback had a limo. He was with friends. He was trying to do the right things. And he still got targeted. Guys have to know that sometimes it doesn't matter what you do — there's always something out there that could harm you, but you should still diligently prepare yourself.

"A well-known teacher of spirituality once said that your character is the sum total of your habits. Your habits are the sum total of your choices. Making the right choices strengthens your good habits, while poor choices only diminish them."
David L. Brown

I saw a January 2009 interview done by an ESPN reporter, interviewing an infamous former Dallas Cowboy defensive back and punt returner shortly after the athlete's release by the Dallas Cowboys. The ESPN reporter asked the athlete why he felt the need to go to a nightclub to drink.

The athlete responded, it was because he was an alcoholic. I commend that athlete for admitting his alcoholism and entering himself into a facility and program to help him conquer his repetitive demons. However, I strongly believe he

76

had two choices on the day he decided to go to the nightclub. One, he made the choice to go, two, he made the choice to drink and get drunk.

Now, my question is this: why did the athlete feel he had to go to a nightclub to drink? He could have made a better choice by deciding to stay home and get drunk on his living room couch, thus avoiding all the legal trouble he found himself in. Plus, police officers are not going to come to his house and arrest him for getting drunk in the privacy of his own home. He made poor decisions that day, which will ultimately and collectively decide his professional career in the NFL.

Chapter 10

We All Make Mistakes

Do you think the coach is going to tag along with you while you're clubbing to make sure you stay out of trouble? Nope. How about the owner of the pro team you play for? No way. Maybe the athletic director of your college team? Not a chance. The point is, you must be responsible for yourself — period.

The dictionary defines a mistake as "an error in action, opinion, or judgment caused by poor reasoning, carelessness, and insufficient knowledge." In other words, most mistakes are not intentional. They result from lack of training, experience, knowledge — or just plain stupidity. I believe that every mistake is an opportunity. When a player makes a mistake, they should ask themselves these questions:

1. What can I do to keep this from happening again?
2. What did I learn from this mistake?
3. If I don't want to make this mistake again, what do I need to change?

If you make a mistake, can you recover, redeem yourself, and rebuild your career? Maybe. Our country is forgiving and open-minded to second chances. However, if you make repeated, unacceptable bad choices, any future opportunities to continue your career could be limited. It's a privilege to play your sport, not a given. Why put yourself, your family, your teammates, and your league through all that anguish and embarrassment? In today's sports society, it's not enough just to be good on the field and court — you have to be good off it as well.

Chapter 11

Parenting an Athlete

"As a parent, I vow to instill in my children the basics of character, humility, kindness, a good attitude, giving back, helping others, having their own faith and spirituality, integrity, and being their own persons to create the life they want for themselves, on and off the field and court."

David L. Brown

For Dads on teaching their child athletes about character...

"Dads, teach them to play with courage, sportsmanship, passion, character, and work ethic. Then

80

watch them strive to be the best, on and off the field and court.

David L. Brown

For Moms on teaching their child athletes about character...

"Moms, teach them patience, respect, integrity, responsibility, and self-confidence. Then watch them grow as a person and athlete."

David L. Brown

For coaches/role models on teaching character to children and players on all athletic levels...

"Coach, teach them discipline, purpose, focus, mental toughness, and perseverance. Then watch them shine and become good people and athletes."

David L. Brown

Chapter 12

You Can Make a Difference

Throughout their careers, many fine athletes who have worked hard and behaved responsibly have quietly sacrificed — in wins, playoff opportunities, possibly even Super Bowls, due to the irresponsibility of teammates. They may not come out and say that publicly — so I did.

True Story, 2008, Youngstown, Ohio

Recently, on an early Saturday morning, I drove a local, high profile high school athlete to one of the nightclubs in our area. He is currently being recruited to continue his athletic career by Ohio State, Pitt, Michigan,

Penn State, and Notre Dame, among others. I didn't tell him where we were going, but I did tell him I had an important point I wanted to make and that it would be up to him to choose to ignore it or consider it.

We stood outside the club and chatted for a moment. He then asked, "So, what are we doing HERE?"

I told him to look closely at the building, to study it for a while. I then asked him to name me five POSITIVE things that would enhance his life and athletic career by walking through the doors of that club someday, or any other club on any given Friday or Saturday night.

He thought for a moment and then smiled, at which time I asked him to exclude "hot babes" from the list, because he can mingle with attractive, professional, grounded, intelligent women at better venues than nightclubs and bars.

After making that exclusion, he could not name one positive thing that could enhance his life and athletic career in any positive way. What he did come up with was a long list of NEGATIVE headline grabbing, career killing, home life destroying, personal and family heartache that he may never be able to fully recover from.

My message to him was clear. Do not put yourself in that position.

Going clubbing is never — let me repeat this — going clubbing is NEVER going to impress the coach (who'll be the one the media hammers all season long with questions about you and your lack of making good choices if something bad happens). If trouble finds you, it won't increase your marketing and earning potential when a company may want to hire you to pitch their products. It won't help you gain respect from teammates who may privately think you're a jerk. It will never impress the team owner who gave you that big contract. It will never cause young kids to worship you (who later will be disappointed and stop wearing your jersey, and whose parents will then despise you). And it will never help you gain respect within your family and community. Your legacy is essentially etched in stone and when your playing days are over, people won't remember your amazing skills and accomplishments — they'll remember the negative headlines.

Is it worth giving it all up for a few hours of fun at a club, bar, or late night party? And, by the way, if you happen to have, or some day will have, a club built into the lower level of your home — the same principles apply.

"Character Durability: an athlete's ability to demonstrate high character and moral conduct consistently throughout their entire career on and off the field and court."
David L. Brown

Chapter 13

It's All About Respect

Winter, 2008

I took a drive to a local police department located in my nearby area. My mind was on research, specifically reality versus perception. I wanted to talk to officers coming out of the building to get some insights about reasons that would cause people to act violently. This is what I found out.

Time and again, the number one reason officers gave me was the perception of being…DISRESPECTED.

The Dictionary defines the word "Disrespect" this way:

1. An expression of lack of respect.

2. A disrespectful mental attitude.

3. A manner that is generally disrespectful and contemptuous.

4. Have little or no respect for or hold in contempt.

Being disrespectful or "dissed" may make one feel devalued as a human being. A guy at a club you encounter may "feel" like you just spit in his face, even though you didn't. It's perception we're talking about here. Perception can be a dangerous and deadly reality from another person's standpoint in regard to you and clubbing. Disrespect is, in my opinion, the worst athlete attitude to have. It is your enemy when dealing with people at clubs, bars, and parties. If you want trouble with another dude, just have him "perceive" that you're dissing him and see how quickly stuff can happen. I commend our athletes. Most mind their own business when they go out and don't often look for trouble but, unfortunately, things do happen sometimes.

Did you know #1:

A recent police study on guns concluded that officers who waited longer between practicing their shooting skills were found to be much slower in their reaction time when drawing their weapon in the real world. The study revealed it generally takes a longer time to react to a situation, and then draw the gun. Even if you carry a gun and can quickly draw it, your accuracy may be minimal. A gun can easily get tangled up in your clothing and then...pop, pop, pop — you could be dead. So make the right choice, use common sense, and don't carry.

Did you know #2:

During research with the local police, I asked them: Where's the best place on a person's body to take a bullet if they had to? The leg? No. Head? Certainly not. Buttocks? No. Abdomen? No. Chest. No way. Neck? Are you kidding? Shoulder? No, too close to the neck. Back? No...a bullet can pierce through your back, back to front, damaging vital organs along the way. Answer: The arm. Why? Because there are no vital organs nearby to cause sudden life-threatening damage.

Okay, so you get the message of this book, right? Now what?

Number one, be a steward of good character and use common sense everywhere you go. Be prepared for anything, but don't put yourself in situations that could be potentially dangerous or deadly. Like in sports, you arrive at camp and work on fundamentals of the game, honing your skills along the way. Your personal safety fundamentals should be honed with the same attitude. Continue to treat others with respect. Surround yourself with good energy and positive people. I want to help make clubbing safe for you, your friends, and your family, before, during, and after.

Chapter 14

If Clubbing You Must — Club Responsibly.™

It's time to make a plan. A clubbing plan. A plan of action. Action that you MUST take to make your life safer. Gain back your peace of mind and confidence. Make good decisions — consistently.

As an athlete, you're physical. It's been that way practically your entire life. Your physicality on the field and court personifies who you are and what you do. It's almost a part of your DNA. Without it, you would not be the player you are. My point is, it's very difficult to turn that off when the game is over. That physical nature you have come to depend on generally stays with you away from the game. It is what it is. That being said, it can be used against you, and you can contribute to it being used against you, but you have a choice to allow it to happen or not.

There are two main ways to get negative headlines in sports off the field and court. One, you act a fool. Two, the other guy acts a fool. It doesn't matter if you're an All-Pro, future Hall of Famer, an athlete on the practice squad, sitting at the end of the bench in basketball, a college All-American, or a walk-on. If you make a poor decision, it will generate significant media attention for you, your family, your teammates, your coaches — the entire organization. It's one of the worst trickle-down effects in sports. It starts with you, and the choices you make.

Part Two

Part Two

Chapter 15

Introducing POPS

What They Are, and How They Could Save Your Life

PO'd Points™ (POPS), are the understated silent club killer. I want to begin by informing you I believe a PO'd Point (POP) is very different from anger. A POP is calm, sneaky, calculated, and thought out. It's usually acted upon over a period of time, rather than the immediate angry outburst we're accustomed to hearing about.

A person who encounters an athlete at a club and exhibits a POP may feel inferior in some way to the athlete. He may perceive an athlete as "bigger than life." To bring that athlete down to their personal "comfort zone," they may pull a gun, a knife, or confront them in order to, in their mind, "humanize" the athlete.

POPS are silent killing cousins to anger.

The dictionary defines anger as: A strong passion or emotion of displeasure or antagonism, excited by a real or supposed injury or insult to one's self or others, or by the intent to do such injury. To excite to anger; to enrage; to provoke. A strong feeling of displeasure and belligerence aroused by a wrong; wrath; ire. A strong feeling of displeasure or hostility.

We all know there are varying degrees of anger. The first definition is extremely important, and one that every athlete should be aware of. Let me repeat a key point, then expand on how it could contribute to being a life or death situation for an athlete. "A strong passion or emotion of displeasure or antagonism, excited by a REAL OR SUPPOSED injury to one's self or others, or by the intent to do such injury.

Recall the information I spoke on earlier about the definition of disrespect, or being "dissed." Disrespect and

PO'd Points are definitely related, yet keenly different. Most of us can easily tell when someone is externally ANGRY. Anger generally accompanies telltale body language, screaming, yelling, flailing arms, obscenities, etc. You basically know when someone is angry.

But PO'd Points often start internally. They can be sneaky, and a person doesn't even have to show any facial expression or body language to indicate they're PO'd. Even a simple smirk on one's face is no indication, but you should pay attention to it. A person doesn't have to look "PO'd" in order to feel that way based on their own internal "perception," real or imagined, of being disrespected in some way.

PO'd Points can be every bit as dangerous as any level of anger. I think people sometimes assume that a person has to be clearly physically angry in order to cause them to act violently. Not true. A person could very well shoot you just because they're simply "PO'd" in a calm way. You never know what a person's anger threshold is. You

97

don't know what little thing could push them over the edge.

My tips and techniques will educate athletes on general "tendencies" of people at clubs, bars, parties, or anywhere else. I'll also educate you on how to recognize them, avoid them, and stay safe.

POPS is all about consistent awareness and using common sense. Protecting yourself and staying safe starts with your mind, first and foremost. The same way you prepare for the next game should be the same way you prepare yourself and your friends BEFORE you go clubbing. It's very important not to become complacent with your awareness and your security plan while clubbing. You must use my tips and techniques on a consistent basis for success.

Chapter 16

Before Clubbing

"It's not always easy to do the right thing, but do it anyway. It could save your life."

David L. Brown

1.   Have the right attitude. Just as you put on your "game face," put on your "club face." When your buddy calls and wants you to go clubbing with him, make sure he understands that you have a "game plan" for the evening to keep everybody safe — just in case. Explain your clubbing safety plan in detail to everyone you know will be with you. Make sure they take it seriously.

2. Understand the moment you step outside your home, you're an instant public figure and a potential target.

3. Leave your best bling at home. Go clubbing in a minimal amount of jewelry you can afford to lose, to avoid standing out. Same with your vehicle. The less bling your vehicle has, the better.

4. Inform at least two to three other friends or family where you're going in case you need a ride afterward, or your vehicle is blocked, or some fool decides to mess with you. Make sure they have your cell number. If you can't reach them in person, leave a voice mail.

5. Know who your friends and family members are friends with. Don't be afraid to ask them who their friends are if you don't know them and have never met them, or maybe met them briefly once or twice. Will they be meeting you at the club later? Will they come by your house and later leave with you and your other friends? Will they

bring other people you may or may not know with them?

6.   Invite friends and family strong enough to tell you...NO! You're an athlete, maybe a high-profile athlete. You may have gotten used to having your way without anyone in your inner private circle questioning your decisions. Take those who will tell you you've had too much to drink, and WILL take your keys from you. It could save your life. You want to surround yourself with people who truly care for you, not enablers. What's an enabler? One who enables another to persist in self-destructive behavior by providing excuses, or by helping that individual avoid the consequences of such behavior.

7.   Call each club you may attend in advance, or have your security or a friend do this for you. Ask the owner or manager if there is a section for VIPs, and where it's located — ground floor, top floor, front of the building, back of the building? Ask in

advance if there is a side or back door where "celebrities" can enter and exit. Yes, athletes are celebrities.

8. Guns. Don't carry them with you! But if you absolutely feel you must, be legal, licensed, and properly trained to use it. Carrying a loaded weapon can cause more potential harm than it can keep you safe. A loaded weapon can cause an already escalated situation to get out of control and become deadly.

9. Let your security person carry a gun if you feel the need. Make sure your security people are also licensed and properly trained. I highly recommend clubbing with TWO professionally trained security people. It's not enough just to have a bodyguard, you have to have a plan. Even though you may have security with you, your number one protector is...YOU! Don't slack on yourself and let your guard down for a moment!

10. Consider purchasing an armored vehicle that you keep at home at all times — really. Consider it an investment. If you're going clubbing with a group of people, make arrangements ahead of time to travel to and from the club in an armored limousine. If the President rides in one, you should too. You're not the President, but you are the president of your own life and athletic career.

11. Know beforehand what routes you're taking to the club AND back home. Take the quickest one available, and make sure they're different. Huddle with your security team, friends and family, to make sure everyone is on the same page.

12. Inside your house. Before you walk out the door, spend a few moments gazing around the house, and remember how things are situated and located. For example, is your master bedroom door open or closed when you leave? Is the light on or off in the kitchen? Is the light on or off in the front entryway? Taking a mental picture of

how your house looks inside as you walk out the door will be important for when you return home. Also, if you had friends over earlier, or someone was working on the house inside or out, make sure all the windows are locked. It's easy for someone to unlatch a window and return later. Living in a gated community complete with security cameras, so that every face entering the grounds can be identified, is also strongly suggested.

13. Outside the house. Will you be leaving a front patio/porch light on? Is the back yard well lit? If you have kids and it's summer, are their bikes still in the yard? If it's winter, take time to view your own tire and footprints as you pull out of your driveway, whether you're backing out or not. Are yours the only set of tire tracks when you leave? Maybe friends or family stopped by earlier…that's fine, just know that. Make sure you close the garage door and remember you closed it.

Make sure the side garage door is also locked. It's all about awareness and common sense.

14. Outside perimeter. Check or have your security people thoroughly check the perimeter of your home. Some fool could be waiting in the shrubs for you to leave. Don't just focus on the ground level...look up into the trees, on the roof, and check the other side of perimeter fences, if you have them.

15. Make sure you activate your home alarm system before you walk out the door!

16. Carry only one credit card to pay for food, tips, or other items. Keep things simple. Carry a small amount of cash with you, because you don't want to be seen pulling out a large wad of cash, which could draw unwanted attention and increase your chances of becoming a target. Leave the house a little earlier than you normally would. You don't want to be predictable in your routine.

17. Once you walk out the door and enter your vehicle, make sure you lock the house doors behind you. Don't speed off in a hurry to get to the club. Drive slowly while leaving your neighborhood. Be keenly aware of who is on the streets and what their demeanor may be. Notice who may be walking on foot and if they're intentionally trying to avoid being noticed in any way. Notice cars parked on the street near your home that you may not recognize.

18. Drive through your neighborhood. Stop somewhere a couple of blocks away, wait ten minutes, then backtrack to your house as if you forgot to get something. Again, be aware who's walking on the streets or vehicles you have never seen before. Do not pull into your driveway, just slowly drive by. If your intuition tells you all is fine, then carry on and proceed to your club destination… safely. If anything seems suspicious,

call the police. Be observant, but don't try to take matters into your own hands.

19. On your way to the club, realize that many people who will also attend have been drinking alcohol and/or doing drugs long BEFORE they arrive. So, before they even get there, they're likely already intoxicated, high, or both.

20. Consider the construction of the building you'll be attending, especially if it's more than one story high. Is the building new? Old? Is it structurally safe? How do you know? If you knew a bridge was deficient, would you drive over it? I bet you wouldn't, and neither would I. No one ever thought the Dallas Cowboys indoor practice facility would collapse on Saturday, May 2, 2009, seriously injuring a special teams coach, leaving a team scout paralyzed for life, and causing injuries to others. Anything can happen — anytime — anywhere, bad weather or not, which

was determined to be the culprit of that collapse. Be the athlete who's prepared for anything.

21. Don't forget to buckle up on your way clubbing, or you may get pulled over and ticketed for not wearing a seatbelt. Most states now have seatbelt laws, so buckle up!

22. Don't drink alcohol before you go clubbing and then get in a vehicle and drive to a club, party, or bar. If you do, you are asking for trouble — and it will find you. There is no acceptable level of alcohol consumption that makes it safe to drive — ever.

23. The bad guys don't always need guns to do damage in your life. Your social security number or a pre-approved credit card application from your trash, could be all they need. Be extra careful with your personal information in your home, and away. Identity theft is the nation's fastest growing crime according to FBI statistics, and identity theft/fraud is the fastest growing category of

Federal Trade Commission (FTC) complaints. Don't be the next victim — protect yourself.

24.   Think of your personal safety as preventative maintenance. You work out during the off-season. You train and stay in shape so you can avoid wear and tear on your body and reduce injuries during the season. POPS is the same way — you have to train your mind, change any bad habits, and prepare yourself each and every time you're in the public's eye.

25.   For more information on purchasing armored vehicles:

http://www.iacarmormax.com

http://www.armoredcars.com

http://www.armoured-vehicles.com

http://www.bukkehave.com

Chapter 17

While Clubbing

"One of life's most painful moments comes when we must admit that we didn't do our homework, that we are not prepared."

Merlin Olsen, former NFL great

1. Check your ego at the door.

2. When you go clubbing, you're NOT attending a club full of your peers, meaning other athletes. The majority of the folks are everyday people, working everyday jobs, with everyday problems and issues. Expect somebody to eventually act a

fool when you go clubbing — just have your POPS plan ready when it happens.

3. Don't be fooled or seduced by a club located in a nice neighborhood or area. Bad things can still happen. Don't assume you're totally safe in the V.I.P. section either. You still always have to be aware of potential danger and not let your guard down.

4. The parking lot. Just like when you go to the mall or store, you exit your vehicle, you take a few steps, then intuitively turn around to take a mental photo of where your car is parked. The same principle applies when clubbing. Remember where the car is parked.

5. Valet parking. Ask the valet attendant the location he/she will be parking your vehicle. Take the time and wait for them to park it, and take a mental photo of where it's located. It wouldn't hurt to get the valet's name also.

6.   You want your security people to conduct themselves like the security people you see on the sidelines at your games. You know, the folks wearing the bright college or pro security shirts or vests that face the stands the whole game? Even if there's a last-second touchdown, or a shot to win the game, they are trained to NOT turn and watch the action. Their job is to watch the crowd in the stands at all times. Your security people should have the same focus. Their job is to watch the crowd in the parking lot, inside the club, and when leaving the club. Their job is NOT to dance, drink, and party with everybody else. Their job is to protect YOU — period.

7.   Inside the club, always maintain a positive attitude and be nice. It sounds simple, but you'll be amazed how positive the results will be. The bad guys will tend to want to mess with you if you come off arrogant and disrespectful. Confidence is a deterrent.

8.   You're a celebrity — and to a degree, an entertainer. Give each person you happen to encounter a quick moment of your highest energy level. When approached for autographs and hellos, look them in the eye, smile, shake hands, then quickly be on your way.

9.   Statistics show, as the night wears on, the chances of an escalated incident increases dramatically. Do not leave when the club or bar closes! Make it a part of your safety plan to leave well before closing.

10.   The two words I mentioned earlier, that could save your life, when encountering someone, are... "I'm sorry," or "I apologize," "My bad," "My fault" — however you want to say it. This is a very important part of your POPS "club etiquette" safety plan. As simple as it may sound, take this seriously. You want to avoid a potential problem, not ignite one.

11. Athletes can use my techniques to dramatically minimize your role and contribution in a potentially dangerous situation. For example, if you encounter someone who's been drinking and you happen to bump into him/her on the dance floor by accident or elsewhere, or they accidentally bump into you, if they seem agitated, tell them immediately — "I'm sorry." DO NOT wait for him/her to do this. You take the initiative! Be the bigger person. Sometimes you have to swallow your pride to stay alive.™

12. You want to say "I'm sorry" at least SIX TIMES — repeatedly. Why? Because when a person is in the early stages of POPS, drinking, annoyed, and maybe incoherent, he won't likely hear you say it the first three times, because he might be too busy running his mouth talking junk back at you. You have to say it at least six times in order for him to truly listen. Be sincere when you say it. You could say something like, "I'm sorry, man, my

bad." or "I apologize, my fault." Let him know you're cool with things, and wait for confirmation that he is too, then quickly walk away, or move to another part of the dance floor. You may not see him as a threat to YOU — but he might see you as a threat to HIM.

13. If someone recognizes you're an athlete, give him an autograph ONLY if he requests one, take a quick photo ONLY on request. Do it QUICKLY and be on your way! Do Not linger for half-an-hour talking about last night's game. Your focus is to stay safe while you're at the club. As an athlete, you easily recognize momentum changes in a game. The ebb and flow of a guy's POPS, who's been drinking, can be difficult to quickly recognize — unless you use my techniques. You are never going to know 100% what someone is going to do and when. You can't get into their minds to see how they tick. But you CAN equip and prepare yourself for the worst.

14. Don't be confused about the difference between being a random, or non-random target. Realize that you CAN, unknowingly or not, contribute to someone acting a fool toward you. Do not allow yourself to get into a verbal battle with anyone. Don't talk back to people, glare at them in a disrespectful manner, or make any perceived negative gestures. It's not worth it, and can escalate very quickly. Always treat people with respect, even though they may not return the courtesy.

15. Alcohol and clubbing. Less is better. None is best™. Use common sense and set boundaries. Don't even think about driving if you've been drinking!

16. Women and clubs. The ladies can definitely be a potential distraction to your clubbing safety plan, and cause you to lose focus. Treat women you meet with respect at all times. After all, she's someone's daughter — possibly a young child's

mother. Ask yourself what your true plan is for the evening. Are you going clubbing to meet women, or are you going with your girlfriend, wife, or significant other? Maybe you just want to relax and have a good time without hassles or drama? Know your reasons, and be honest. If you go clubbing with the intent to meet and leave with a woman, be certain she didn't come with her man. He could show up later unexpectedly, or another man could become interested in her too. Testosterone and alcohol can be dangerous and deadly when mixed with competition for women at clubs, bars, and parties. What might be her motive for hooking up with you? Is it the lure and excitement of meeting, then leaving with a high profile college or pro athlete? Is she looking for a long-term relationship? A possible financial windfall? A short-term fling? A one-night rendezvous? Don't forget to consider sexually transmitted diseases and AIDS. Have a smart safety plan for sex, if that's your intent. Be responsible. Protect yourself — and her.

17. Leaving the club. When you are ready to leave, before closing, position yourself in the middle of your two security people. Why? They will provide a shield for you. Walk through and out of the building at a preferable distance of at least three feet between you and them, back to front. If anyone tries to get to you for a last minute autograph or some fool wants to act crazy, you'll be insulated between two big bodies. Don't slack on positioning and distance. Just like in a game, if you're not in the right position, it's difficult to execute the offense and defense. Try to leave as quietly and unnoticed as possible. This includes your friends or family. You don't want to draw unnecessary attention to yourself by being loud.

18. Make sure all friends or family are accounted for. If they decide to stay, be aware of it, and find out how they'll get back home if they rode with you.

Make arrangements to have someone else pick them up, if needed. You don't want to backtrack to the club later to pick anyone up, if you can help it. That's too risky.

19. Make sure not to leave your cell phone, Blackberry, or anything else at the club important enough to have to go back for — especially anything that would contain personal contact information, like addresses and phone numbers.

20. At clubs, bars, and parties, don't accept a drink from anyone except a bartender, and observe the drink being mixed. Don't leave your drink unattended or share drinks, because someone might slip a drug into it that will make you unconscious or sick, and vulnerable to assault. If you are in doubt about a drink, get a new one, or just don't drink at all.

Chapter 18

After Clubbing

"Only in growth, reform and change, paradoxically enough, is true security to be found."

Anne Morrow Lindbergh

1.   Leaving the club. You want to always leave well BEFORE closing, at least two hours.

2.   Be aware of your surroundings when you're outside the club. Scan the area and get a quick sense of the vibe outside, the number of people lingering, and noise and argument levels. For example, be aware if bouncers are having trouble

clearing the parking lot because of drunk people. Avoid distractions like talking and texting on your cell phone when leaving.

3. Leave quickly. Do Not linger outside the club or bar talking to people, signing autographs, taking photos, etc. Remember where your vehicle is parked after taking that earlier mental photo, or get to the valet quickly, get in your vehicle when it arrives, put your seatbelt on — and leave.

4. If a friend or family are at home, make a quick call to let them know you're on your way there.

5. Be aware if anyone is following you. Your security people and your driver should also be aware of this. Just like you depend on your teammates to do their jobs to win a game, you must also depend on and expect your security people and driver to do the same.

6. Police are aware what time clubs and bars close. Their radar is heightened between 1:00 and 3:00 a.m. Drive home at posted speed limits. Don't be

drunk while driving. You will get caught...eventually. It doesn't take much to exceed most state legal limits for DUI and DWI. If you know you've been drinking after clubbing — DON'T DRIVE! Remember the friends you informed earlier of your evening plans? Call them to pick you up if you've been drinking, or call a cab. My motto for athletes is, if you're drinking and driving — you're not striving.™

7.   If you decide to drive (I know you won't), avoid talking and texting on your cell phone, as this causes distractions and can be dangerous, whether drinking or not. Consider a "hands free" option.

8.   Avoid club hopping — going from one club to another. Remember, the later the evening, the higher the risk factors.

9.   Take the quickest route back home, but take a different route than you did on arrival.

10. If you happen to get pulled over by police for ANY reason, my advice — chill, baby, chill!

Cooperate and be professional. If you have nothing to hide and have done nothing wrong, you should be fine. Don't allow your emotions to get the best of you in this situation. You want to get home safely, not spend the night or weekend in somebody's jail.

11.   Arriving home. Home invasion in sports is REAL! When you're driving home, I suggest driving straight home. I apologize if this sounds juvenile, but if the club or bar closed at 3:00 a.m., and you left at 1:00 a.m., stopping somewhere else to have a nightcap, attend another club or party, or even stopping at a restaurant to grab a bite to eat only increases the risks. Why bother? Drunk people are also out clubbing, partying, drinking and driving, and will be frequenting these places too. How many times have you heard about an altercation in a parking lot in the wee hours of the morning? I have — I've seen it.

12. When you arrive back at your neighborhood, drive slowly. Be aware of who may be on foot and what they may be doing.

13. Do not immediately pull into your driveway. Drive slowly past your home, looking intently at the outer perimeters to make sure everything is the same as you left it. Take note of outside lights you left on before leaving. Make sure they're still on. Bad guys like to unscrew light bulbs to avoid being detected. Look at windows carefully, making sure none seem broken or any screens missing or damaged. Look at doors, including garage doors, front and side. Make sure they're not ajar or damaged in any way.

14. Drive around the block again, maybe twice. If things feel good and look good, proceed to return home. If not — call the police.

15. If it's winter, notice if foot and tire prints in the driveway are the same as when you left. If it's not winter or it doesn't snow where you live, outside

front and rear lights, windows and doors will be your initial check points.

16. Once inside the garage, do not immediately get out of your locked vehicle. Leave it running. Check your side and rear view mirrors to ensure the garage door has fully closed behind you and no one has slipped in before it closes.

17. Leave your headlights on for a few moments before exiting, and pay attention to the inside area of your garage and adjoining entry door to the house. Bad guys take light bulbs out inside the garage too. Make sure the inside entry door hasn't been tampered with. If all looks safe and as you left it, then proceed to go inside your home. If not, reopen the garage door — with the vehicle still running and the headlights on, leave quickly, and call the police.

18. Immediately reactivate your home alarm system once inside your home after determining all is fine in the garage.

19.   If you choose to own a gun, your home is the best place to keep it. If it's there, you will become empowered to use it in case an intruder enters or is already inside your house. Use common sense, and by all means protect yourself and your family if you have to. Make certain that any guns, knives, or other weapons inside your home are safely locked away in an area not accessible to youngsters and teens if you have kids.

20.   Pets are great for home security. Dogs, big or small, are wonderful deterrents to home invasion. If you don't have one, consider it. A dog doesn't have to be big and mean to be effective. I used to have a miniature dachshund. On the other side of a closed door, she had the bark and growl of a much larger dog.

21.   Now that you're inside the house, safe and secure, you can relax and get comfortable, right? Wrong. There's still work to be done inside your home. Keep reading for more of inside the house tips

later in the book. As with most things worth doing, the more you apply these clubbing tips and techniques, the better your awareness will become. The more intuitive you are will greatly improve your confidence, help you sleep better at night, and reward you with a sense of control in your life and athletic career.

22.   POPS are about preparation, awareness, and confidence — not fear. Being fearful means you're not prepared. Being prepared and having confidence allows you to make decisions more quickly and correctly in case of trouble. It allows you to keep your emotions at an even keel so you can think clearly and make good choices, even in the midst of a bad situation. Being nervous before, during, and after clubbing is okay. That's not being afraid. It just means you care. You don't have to live in fear. You should always be prepared. POPS is similar to sports — the better prepared you are, and the more you know, the

faster you play in a game. The better decisions you make — the more successfully you'll execute your game plan.

23. If you happen to be walking to or from a destination and you think you're being followed, cross the road and walk confidently to another busy area, shop, business, or well-lit house and call the police.

24. Carjacking is scary and potentially deadly. It is a serious threat to your personal safety. If you are ever confronted by an armed carjacker, don't resist. Give up your keys, money, and jewelry without resistance. Don't argue, fight or chase the guy. You can be seriously injured or killed. Call the police immediately afterward. When driving in the city, make sure windows are rolled up and doors are locked, especially at stop signs and stop lights.

25. Share this book with a teammate, coach, members of your organization, and your agent. College

athletes can also share this book with their school athletic directors. The only way you can help reduce clubbing violence is to continue to educate everyone involved and spread the word.

Chapter 19

More POPS to Be Aware of

1. He's calm. Don't let calmness fool you. It can be dangerous.

2. He has a slight or exaggerated smirk on his face.

3. He walks away and does not immediately retaliate.

4. He's seen shortly thereafter having a discussion with his friends at the club, looking and pointing toward you.

5. He leaves the club area you're in after a short period of time without incident.

6. He's seen back in the area again, acting agitated or suspicious.

7.   He continually tries to make eye contact with you. He could want you to know what's coming, but doesn't want you to know when.

8.   He literally tells you he's coming back later — and does.

9.   He says nothing, does nothing, then leaves, but does not come back into your immediate area. He could possibly be waiting for you somewhere, and attempt to confront you there or follow you in your vehicle when you leave.

10.   He talks smack, curses at you, makes hand gestures, but is not overly agitated or angry at this point. He then leaves, and is nowhere to be seen when you leave the club.

11.   He damages your vehicle outside the club, then leaves. Be careful, he may not be satisfied with damaging your car, and things may escalate at some point later.

12.   He doesn't say anything to you, but tells the friends you came with of his intentions.

13.   He looks you in the eye from a safe distance and seems calm, without saying a word to you. This is when the POPS period is heating up. He's trying to rationalize his own perception of you disrespecting him and how he might react to it. His buddies might be egging him on to "do something about it." Peer pressure is strong at clubs, bars, and parties. Add alcohol, and people feel invincible and fearless. It makes them do stupid things they normally wouldn't do — or maybe they would.

14.   He tries to get information from other people at the club about you and who you came with (security, how many friends, male and female, etc.), in an effort to determine who might be carrying a weapon.

15.   You look in his eyes. Your gut tells you his attitude and demeanor is saying, "Okay, now I'm PO'd."

16. You may think he's smart enough NOT to mess with you in a public place with plenty of witnesses. Maybe. Maybe not. He might have a buddy confront you later that night, or some point in the near future. If there was an incident or war of words between the two of you, maybe nothing escalated. You may have long forgotten about it after a few hours, or couple of days — but he didn't. You might be making a trip to the golf course to play a few holes and some fool steps up on you with a gun. These kinds of bad guys won't wait too long to make their move. Don't take anything for granted — just be prepared for it.

17. He's clearly been drinking and acting a fool.

18. He's clearly been drinking and NOT acting a fool. A mellow drunk dude can be just as dangerous.

19. He wants to be famous or known in the community for messing with you, the athlete. This is his fifteen minutes of fame, his sick legacy, and you're his target. He can't do it without YOU.

20.　He's seen you at a club before, and views it as an opportunity to settle things or make a name for himself. Maybe he just doesn't care what goes down.

21.　Men generally will commit the act of shooting a gun, more so than a woman at a club. If a woman shows POPS, she'll likely have her male friend or boyfriend confront you. Beware of female POPS also!

Ten Perceived POP Reasons

1.　He thinks you looked at him funny. (Really, it doesn't take much.)

2.　He thinks you looked at his woman, were trying to talk to his woman, looked his woman's body up and down, or commented on his woman in a negative or positive way, which he perceived as disrespectful.

3.   He thinks you're in competition with a woman he wants to hook up with. He feels inferior to you, your status as an athlete, your wealth, and fame.

4.   He's had a bad day, bad month, or bad year. He may feel that he has a lousy life, is unhappy, and can't see any daylight. He has a chip on his shoulder and low self-esteem.

5.   He thinks you "dissed" him in some way, shape, or form. It doesn't matter that you feel you didn't do anything wrong. What matters is his perception of being disrespected, real, or imagined.

6.   You're an athlete, he's not. You're wealthy, he's not. You're well known, either in the local community or nationally, he's not. You could have any woman you want, he can't. You live a great life and have tons of opportunities to continue doing so as a college or pro athlete — he doesn't.

7.   He thinks you're another arrogant athlete who believes you can do anything you want and people will still love and cheer for you. He's disgusted with that mentality, but would sell his soul to the devil to trade places with you for a day. Basically — he's desperate. Desperation is dangerous at clubs, bars, and parties — especially when mixed with alcohol or drugs.

8.   He lingers in the parking lot after the club closes, or lingers when you leave the club.

9.   Watch out for groups of people. Bad guys generally like to roll with a group of people. Misery loves company.

10. We, the upstanding public and sports fans, can easily access your salary on the internet — so can the bad guys.

Twenty-five More Clubbing Safety Tips

1. When you're inside clubs or bars, be aware of where rear and side exits are located.

2. The moment you step foot inside that club, reduce your distraction level. This might sound simple, but you'd be amazed at the number of things you get distracted by. Like your cell phone, Blackberry, iPod, or exaggerated conversations with friends.

3. Be aware of people around you on the dance floor and elsewhere. Take note of the vibe they give off. Be keen to people that seem surly, annoyed, or agitated.

4. If the building where you're clubbing has multiple levels, try to stay on the first level. You don't want to waste time taking the elevator or the stairs if trouble breaks out. You want to get out as quickly as possible.

137

5.   If you're clubbing on the first level, don't go too deep inside. Stay within a good distance from the entrance and side or rear exits if you possibly can.

6.   Remember, you want to have a good time, but you also want to have a good safety plan in case a situation occurs.

7.   You should insist your personal security NOT drink at all while clubbing. I've heard one too many fatal stories of personal security losing their focus because they were partying just as hard, if not harder, than their client! Because it is distributed so quickly through the body, alcohol affects the central nervous system, even in small amounts! It also affects several parts of your brain. In general, it contracts brain tissue and depresses the central nervous system. When alcohol reaches the brain, it interferes with communication between nerve cells and can significantly suppress nerve pathways. What does this mean? Alcohol reduces your reaction time —

substantially. That's something you don't want if trouble starts.

8. Before you go to the club, make sure your personal security has been thoroughly trained to respond and effectively handle an escalated situation.

9. Make sure you and your personal security are properly and legally licensed to carry a gun in the state in which you are attending the club. If not licensed in that state, avoid clubbing!

10. If you haven't been properly trained to carry a concealed weapon — c'mon, man, don't carry the weapon on you!

11. You don't have to be a target in order to prepare yourself. You could be enjoying yourself with friends at a club or bar and a situation breaks out with other club goers who have absolutely NOTHING to do with you. Be prepared for other situations not directly related to you, and exit quickly.

12.   If something does break out that is NOT related to you, leave! Don't hang around to find out what happened to who, who said what, who did what and why. Many times tensions are still high, and things can escalate worse AFTER the police or club security gets involved.

13.   When in doubt, don't! If the thought of needing to carry a gun with you to a club, bar, or party makes you feel uneasy — just stay home!

14.   Your attitude is the control center of your life. If you have a good attitude about safety, you'll make the right decisions. Follow my tips and techniques. You'll enjoy a better life, have more confidence, and attain the peace of mind you've been looking for.

15.   You're young, big, strong, tough, and playing at the college, NFL, or NBA level. You may feel invincible. You can easily correct a mistake at practice and in a game, but you might not get a second opportunity when clubbing.

16.   No one deserves to have a gun pulled on them or be shot at just because you might look at someone funny, or talk trash to them at a club, bar, or party. If something bad does go down, you may have contributed to that incident in some way without even knowing it.

17.   Your first and most important contribution to an incident like that may be to avoid clubbing in the first place. If clubbing you must — club responsibly.

18.   DO NOT follow a woman back to her place after clubbing. Do not drive a woman back to your place either — no matter what! This could be deadly in a heartbeat. If you met her the night of clubbing and you both choose to leave together, that's fine, you're adults. However, you might not be aware of other circumstances you could encounter once you get to her place, or yours. There could be a jealous ex-boyfriend, a husband you didn't know about, a guy she met at the club,

bar, or party that same night. Someone could be targeting you, waiting. He might have followed you to her place, or her to yours. You can imagine the increased chances of someone getting seriously injured or killed in this situation. Throw in alcohol (again), maybe drugs, high emotions, guns, and you now have yourself a distasteful recipe for potential disaster.

19.   Well, you say, maybe a nice hotel room would be a better choice? I don't believe so. Again, too dangerous. It's just not worth the risk these days — and you're smarter than that, right? I know you are.

20.   Due diligence and women. Due diligence is a term you must be familiar with — now. It is used for a number of concepts. We'll focus on the "people" concept of the term. It involves the voluntary performance of an investigation of a person or persons. It refers to the care a reasonable person (you) should take before

entering into an agreement with another party (her). Due diligence is a way of preventing unnecessary harm to you. Here's a sports example. Your coaching staff conducts due diligence on the next opponent in an attempt to uncover tendencies that can be exploited to your team's advantage in the course of a game. What advantage is uncovered from clubbing due diligence for you? Staying alive. Sometimes you win, sometimes you lose. Make sure you know who you're waking up to the next morning.

21. Athletes, if you're tempted or enticed to talk smack with someone at a club, bar, or party — DON'T. Save that for your next game. If you choose to allow yourself to become distracted and lose focus in a game, it may cost your team a win. If you allow yourself to get distracted and lose focus clubbing — it could cost you your life.

22. People at clubs, bars, and parties don't tend to settle their differences with their fists anymore.

These days they carry guns or knives. They will use them without any regard for your well being whatsoever.

23.   Your physical size and strength are no longer an obstacle for the bad guys. They use guns as their equalizer these days.

24.   What's your best defense when clubbing? Your mind. Who's your mind's best friend? Your attitude.

25.   Worry is of your own creation, perceived or otherwise. Fear is nothing more than the response you have chosen. When athletes have the proper tools, preparation, and the right attitude, fear and worry are minimized. Choose to be aware. Choose to be informed. Choose to prepare and stay safe the right way — and continue to play the game you love.

POPS allows you, the athlete, to change your previous nightlife habits for the better. You're simply not going to allow anyone to push your emotions over the edge, which would be detrimental to you, your family, your team, and your league, right? POPS teaches you how to lay a good foundation for all nightlife experiences. As athletes, you have to THINK about security, and security needs to be a focal part of your safety plans for your entire career.

Chapter 20

Twenty-five Stayin' Alive Safety Tips

1. Make it a point to thoroughly research clubs and bars. (Due diligence.) Choose those that stress the importance of ID checks at the door. Teens trying to sneak into clubs and bars with fake IDs are likely to cause trouble if they do get in.

2. Choose clubs and bars that invest in discretely placed security cameras. Whether cameras are located inside or out, they are a major deterrent to trouble.

3. Keep eyes and ears open — and hands free. It is important to be alert to who and what is around you. Headphones or earbuds may give the

impression that you are less aware. Headphones also cut you off from your surroundings and make it very easy for an attacker to sneak up on you, so keep the headphones and earbuds off, inside and outside.

4. When driving, if you, or someone who's driving you, believe you're being followed, reverse your direction — it will take them a much longer time to turn around, and they will likely just continue on to find a different target.

5. If you're ever in a situation where a bad guy pulls out a gun (I pray not), run away in a zigzag pattern. Look for cover, but mostly concentrate on gaining distance. Putting distance between you gives you protection against weapons. How? It is difficult for even the best marksman to hit a moving target, so be a moving target. Hitting anything more than fifteen yards away is difficult. By pulling a weapon he has threatened your life, and you must believe he means it. Get out of the

situation before he completes his threat. The odds are more on your side with every yard you gain in distance.

6. Practice your POPS clubbing safety plan. In an emergency, the mind is often frozen with indecision. The body carries through if you have practiced or trained for this emergency. Practice often, out loud. Practice what you need to do in every detail. Include your friends and family too.

7. Keep your head up and look confident when you're walking anywhere. Your posture can make all the difference in how you are perceived by a potential attacker. If you are looking down, seem distracted, or look afraid, you are more likely to become a target. Why? An attacker makes you as an easy target when your body language tells him that you are fearful. Keep your head up, be aware of what is going on around you, and keep your gaze fixed at nose level.

8.   Have your keys ready at all times when you approach your vehicle. Check inside your vehicle first, before entering. Do this even if driving a short distance.

9.   While traveling in your vehicle and coming to a stop, leave enough room to maneuver around other cars. Drive in the center lane if it's available. Avoid driving alone. Don't stop to assist strangers.

10.   When parking and leaving your vehicle, never leave valuables in plain view. Always look around before you get out. Make sure you lock the doors and the windows are rolled up.

11.   While approaching your vehicle, be sure to walk with purpose, and stay alert.

12.   Beware of "Bump and Run" scenario. No...not that bump and run technique a cornerback operates with. I mean, a car, usually with a driver and at least one passenger, rear ends or "bumps" you in traffic. You quickly get out to check the

149

damage and exchange information. Either the driver or one of the passengers in the other car jumps in your car and drives off or attempts to rob you. If bumped by another vehicle, make sure there are other cars and vehicles around before getting out of your car. If the situation leaves you uneasy, write down the plate number (if visible) and the car's description, and motion the other car to follow you. Drive to the nearest police station or well-lighted area. Always take your keys with you when leaving your vehicle.

13. At home, experience reveals three basic concepts repeatedly: The appearance that an occupant is present and is attentive to the condition of the property is, in itself, a potent deterrent to would-be criminals. Physical security equipment is worthless unless used. The component in any security system most likely to fail is the human one. Keeping your residence well kept and giving the appearance of being home (being in and out,

and active inside) is the first fundamental step toward preventing crime there.

14.   When in a parking lot, look at the cars parked on either side of your vehicle. If a male in a vehicle is sitting alone in the seat nearest your car, or if you are parked next to a van, always enter your car from the side opposite the other vehicle.

15.   If you have encountered a violent situation, the most important thing is to react immediately. If the bad guy has a gun but you are not under his control, take off running! Experts say he will only hit you, a running target, four out of every one hundred shots. And, even then, it most likely will not be a vital organ, so don't be afraid to RUN — it's okay.

16.   Make nonthreatening eye contact. It may be your first instinct to lower your gaze as you walk to and through a club, bar, or party. Looking straight into the face of potential bad guys is the better

option. Eye contact may scare him off because he may fear you'll be able to identify them later.

17.   Believe in yourself. When you believe in yourself, you'll trust your wisdom and your mental strength. You'll trust your perceptions, and you'll believe you have the right to your emotional and physical well-being.

18.   Understand the reality — and face it. Many athletes understand the realities of nightlife but some don't face it full on. Completely see and accept reality and you'll be miles closer to being safe and being in charge of your life.

19.   Trust your intuition. If you forget everything you learned from this book, remember this one thing — if your intuition alarm goes off, there IS something wrong. Trust it, and act upon it to increase your personal safety.

20.   Focus on what you CAN do. Athletes have the power to make a difference through daily actions. While you cannot control every outside

circumstance, you can choose how you respond to them.

21.   Stay calm under pressure. How can athletes stay calm if they find themselves under pressure and make better decisions? It is normal for most people, let alone athletes, to get upset and overwhelmed when they feel under pressure. When you are centered, you are most able to assess the situation, figure out what your options are, and make thought out decisions rather than just reacting. So keep your emotions in check.

22.   Protect yourself from a threat. Self-defense includes more than knowing how to hit or kick. It also includes knowing skills and behaviors that can prevent a problem in the first place. For effective self-defense, pay attention to your tone of voice and choice of words. Pay attention to your body language and facial expressions. Projecting an attitude of awareness and confidence is a powerful clubbing self defense

skill. Are you glaring at someone and making disrespectful gestures? This makes you look like an aggressor. Most communications with others will work best if your body is upright and your face is calm. Dealing with a conflict works best if your voice, tone, words, body, and expression are firm, polite, strong and clear.

23.   Protect yourself from an attack. Your first choice is to leave a confrontation, if you can, by simply walking or running away. In an attack, you might have to be willing to risk a possible injury in order to escape. If someone is pointing a gun or waving a knife at you, it is safer to run away most of the time. If someone is grabbing you with a gun to your head, remember that the gun is a lot more dangerous when it is pointed *at* someone rather than *away* from someone. If someone is holding a knife to your throat, you might want to grab the knife, even if it means cutting your hands.

24.   POPS is about being confident and being prepared — not fear. Don't let fear imprison you. I believe personal safety for all athletes is now everybody's business. By setting aside our own discomfort about speaking up, and by risking the displeasure of someone else when we do, we are sending a powerful message to our young athletes that your well being is our top priority.

25.   After you have finished reading this book — go back and read it again! Use it often as a reference point.

Chapter 21

Twenty Away Game Safety Tips

Nothing wrecks getting out and having a good time on a road trip more than getting hurt, robbed, or arrested. When athletes travel on the road, they might not recognize potential dangers that would be obvious to them at home. They may not have the resources that would normally be available to them at home. Different is not wrong, and people in different places have different ways of doing things. If you treat people with respect, kindness and patience, most of them will respond with the same. The good news is that most dangers are avoidable if you keep the following POPS personal safety tips in mind during road games.

1.   Be proactive. Carry this book with you to away games — you'll be happy you did.

2.   Avoid stress by planning to travel at a relaxed pace instead of hurrying to do everything.

3.   If clubbing on the road, figure out where you are going in advance.

4.   Most times, you are safer with people whom you approach rather than with people who approach you. That said, there are many kinds people you will encounter on the road who might offer their help for various reasons. Thank them, but notice whether they are acting in a way that makes you even a little bit uncomfortable. Is someone just being helpful? Or are they trying to get too close to you? Are they being too pushy? You can interrupt someone and leave politely by saying, "Sorry, gotta go. Thanks!"

5.   Carry yourself with awareness, calmness, and confidence during road games, making sure you notice what is happening around you in all

directions. Don't stare at people, but look around with a "soft eye." Keep assessing your environment if you've got some free time before or after a game. Neighborhoods can change quickly from one block to the next. Places that are safe by day are not always safe by night. Isolated places are usually less safe than places where there are more people around. Places where gangs hang out are to be avoided at all times. You want to stay away from people who might select you as a target because they feel you are on their turf.

6. Move away from people whose behavior is unexpected, especially if it seems to be oriented toward you. Leave ANY TIME you feel uncomfortable. This might mean walking into a shop, crossing the street, leaving a restaurant, mall, bar, or nightclub — or changing your plan and going to where more people are. Your intuition is one of the best tools you have for

protecting your personal safety, as well as at home. Don't ignore it.

7. If you're walking on foot, and anyone, for any reason, starts walking with you and talking, make sure that this is something YOU are choosing. Scan in all directions in case this person has a friend who is approaching from behind you. You can disengage by going into a store or by saying firmly, "Sorry, no!" or "No thank you!" Use your peripheral vision and keep your awareness on where that person is after they have left your immediate area.

8. If someone tries to pick a fight with you, de-escalate the confrontation. Walk away from insults rather than getting into an argument. If somebody claims you did something wrong, apologize. This does not mean that you agree, but that you are sorry that this person is upset. Remember the POPS "I'm sorry" self defense

technique, and be friendly while you leave, even if the other person is acting a fool.

9. Do what you can to prevent robbery or personal injury, but remember that YOU ARE MORE IMPORTANT THAN YOUR STUFF! Your stuff can be replaced. You cannot. After you have given up your stuff, do not just stand there. Without waiting to see what the robber is going to do next, run to safety. In some places, thieves might try to harm you rather than have you report the robbery.

10. Carry a cell phone that works locally. Any safety plan that involves a cell phone should also have a backup plan. Cell phones, while very convenient, do not always work, and your battery may be weak. Having a backup safety plan that does not rely on cell phones is important for your personal safety when traveling at home or on the road.

11. At your hotel during away games, be able to close securely the places you are sleeping, especially in

hotels. Make sure you can lock the door well from the inside, or use a rubber doorstop. Sometimes, even hotel employees will steal from guests. Think before you open your hotel room door instead of just assuming that the person at the door is safe.

12.   If you feel you must carry a gun with you during away games, know the local laws of the city you're in and respect them. Getting arrested is just not worth it. Check with airlines ahead of time, and make sure you understand the rules about what you can carry with you and what you can't on airplanes.

13.   Let people who care about you know where you are and what you are doing, both for your personal safety during away games, and their peace of mind at home. Give people at home your itinerary and how to get hold of you. Let them know when your plans change. Call family members or other people who might worry about

you. Emotional safety for the people who love you lies in their knowing that you are okay. Taking a few minutes to give someone who might be worrying about you the gift of peace of mind is just plain smart.

14.   Forget the "it won't happen to me" attitude. It CAN happen to you. Don't allow yourself to be in denial.

15.   Preventing clubbing violence is not the only area in an athlete's life where getting help makes a difference. Whether you are dealing with a personal safety issue or facing any other challenge, knowing how to ask for help from others is a fundamental life skill. Even though it may feel that way sometimes, it is important to remember that you are not alone. You do not need to reinvent the wheel. You do not need to face problems by yourselves. By reading this book and applying the tips and techniques I have listed, athletes can bring more protection, comfort,

information, resources, and understanding into your lives.

16.	Why bother learning about safety? Fed up with feeling uneasy every time you think about going clubbing with friends? Do you feel afraid because off all the terrible headlines you've heard and read about regarding other athletes, maybe even a teammate? How would you feel if you were more confident about your ability to stay emotionally and physically safe? What would your life be like? POPS teaches you how to protect your emotional and physical safety and can change your life, because the courage, self-respect and power that you need to keep yourself and your family safe, lies within you — it always has.

17.	Now you can fight back by applying POPS tips and techniques when you go clubbing. Applying all your new wisdom makes the possibility of an attack much less likely. But it still might happen.

18. You should not be afraid to ask questions about your personal safety. Seek advice on whom to contact for professional licensed instruction on how to properly use a weapon, if you feel you must carry one, and do so responsibly.

19. Always travel with someone you know and trust when you go clubbing, and make sure you carry your POPS game plan with you. Remember — not many good things happen after midnight.

20. If you're the recipient of a crime while you're playing on the road, don't be embarrassed to report that you have been victimized.

With this book, I wish to instill in all athletes a positive mindset to the highest standards of personal character and moral conduct, from the high school level to the pros, that fans, leagues, and their teams expect from athletes. I hope this book will assist the NCAA, NFL, NBA, UFL, NHL, and MLB in maintaining its value and strong brand for all involved for many years to come.

I encourage leagues, teams, college and university athletic directors, and pro agents, to share POPS™ tips and techniques with their athletes. It's a program that works. POPS can easily be integrated in coordination with their own athlete safety and security programs, to create an even broader safety and security foundation on which to educate and build.

A final note for college and pro teams athletes play for. Preventing a potential problem is far more efficient than fixing a problem afterward. Once a problem occurs, it's far more time consuming and expensive to address it than it is to have a comprehensive game plan like POPS inserted in the first place. POPS helps prevent problems from happening and, in the long run, it saves athletes, teams and organizations money — and it could save a life. Be the change — spread the message.

PLAY HARD. DO GOOD. CharacterAthletic.com™   **Stay in the game — it's your C.H.O.I.C.E.**

About the Author

David L. Brown is founder of Athlete Safety Experts™ (ASE), Character Athletic Safety Academy™ (CASA), and University of Integrity.™

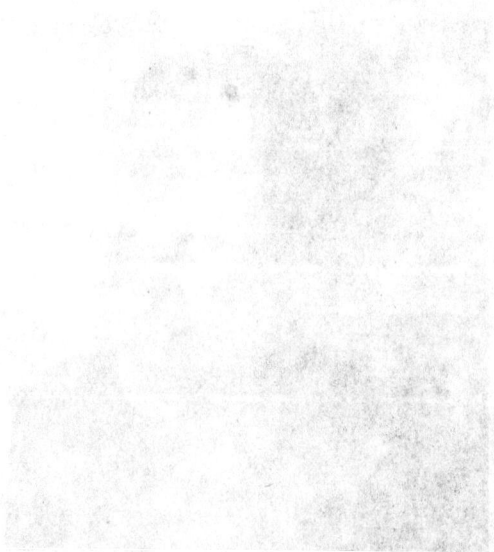

Personal Biography

Early Seventies – In junior high I received honors as a wrestler. I was voted an all-star while playing first base and right field on a team coached by my late dad. I also enjoyed playing my favorite sport — football — on a team with my brother. We lived in a beautiful little beach town in South Haven, Michigan.

During off seasons, to hone my skills in basketball, I attended Hoosier Basketball Camp at Lake James, Angola, Indiana, three years in a row in 1974, 1975, and 1976. Following the conclusion of the 1975 camp, I was honored to be named an all-star, and was the recipient of the "Pride" award, given to the player who exhibited the most effort and intensity during camp. That same year I was voted by the camp counselors to receive the Tom Saylor Award, which recognizes the player who demonstrates an excellent attitude and rapport with other campers, shows intense desire to improve himself, and is exemplary in sportsmanship and conduct. It was quite an honor.

The camps were great fun, and I got to meet, chat with, and get autographs from some of the all-time great players like Bob Lanier, Jerry Sloan, and Bob Love, and college coaches like Fred Schaus of Purdue, Johnny Orr of Michigan, and Tex Winter of Northwestern.

Late Seventies – After my sophomore year in high school, while I still lived in Michigan, my dad worked in a steel mill as a metallurgist and foreman. Shortly thereafter, a lot of plants in our area were beginning to close down permanently due to a bad economy. Unfortunately, Dad's plant succumbed to the poor economy and announced the plant would be closing its doors for good. It was tough on my dad and our family. We loved the area in South Haven, had made long friendships, and both my dad and mom were active in the community.

Dad, or "Pops," as we often called him, had to make some tough choices back then. It was, either keep his family in the area and find another job, or go where the jobs were. He ultimately accepted a pretty good job offer out of state in the New Castle, Pa. area. Our family later relocated to New Wilmington, Pa., a small, quiet town just up the road from New Castle, and home to the Westminster Titans and Westminster College, a private liberal arts college.

At Wilmington High School, I was active in football, basketball, and track & field. I was a 6'-3', 200 pound safety and wide receiver on the football team. After completing my two year stint in New Wilmington, I was honored to graduate as a two-time all tri-county defensive back, and in 1977 was also voted most valuable defensive back.

On the basketball team at Wilmington, I was a center, and considered a "rugged rebounder." I manned the middle, and successfully held my own against taller opponents due to smarts, strong fundamentals, and athletic ability. I played on a few all-star teams, and enjoyed the experiences. In track, I ran 100, 200, 440 meters, and the long jump.

In my senior high school year, I was recruited in football, my best and favorite sport, by the likes of Ohio State, Wisconsin, Louisville, Virginia Tech, and West Virginia University to name a few. My dad, family, and I loved traveling to the cities and touring the campuses. I was classified by college scouts and coaches as a "Blue Chip" athlete coming out of high school.

I was focused on football, track, and basketball, but I lost my focus in the classroom. I was a bright kid, I just didn't apply myself like I should have. Instead, I focused on sports and girls, like many seventeen year olds do.

So, in 1979, after the disappointment of not being able to play for a major college or university, I opted to sign to play football at a local school, Slippery Rock State College, which is now known as Slippery Rock

University, or The Rock, now in NCAA Division II. I majored in communications. The highlight of my brief football career at The Rock was the September 29, 1979 game at the famed Michigan Stadium in Ann Arbor, playing Shippensburg. We lost that game, but it was a great experience.

I later returned to college and earned an English degree from Penn State University.

www.ingramcontent.com/pod-product-compliance
Lightning Source LLC
Chambersburg PA
CBHW070959040426
42443CB00007B/573